The Birds

Berrywood.

Written by

Peter Rennells

Edited by Kirsty Peake

Published by Widecombe History Group.

IBSN no 9781916284920

To Dear Mina

Thankyou so much

Peter

Mina chan

Pere の 本を 送ってあ゛りがとう。
近くに いろの に 会ってなゝぱね—. 今度ゆっくり
会いましょーネ.

from Miho

Plan of Berrywood

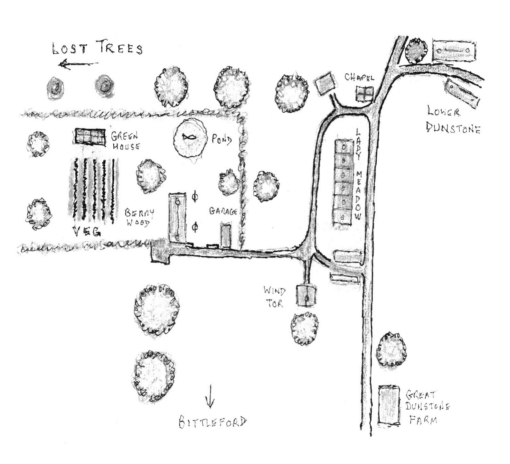

LOST TREES

GREEN HOUSE

POND

CHAPEL

LOWER DUNSTONE

LADY MEADOW

BERRY WOOD

GARAGE

VEG

WIND TOR

BITTLEFORD

GREAT DUNSTONE FARM

Berrywood,
Widecombe in the Moor
Spring/Summer 2020 – Covid-19 Lockdown

Dear Reader

Since retirement I have spent years observing the wildlife that visits Berrywood. Sadly, the bird count has severely reduced over the last few years. Every year in the last 27 I have watched the preparation and departure of vast flights of swallows and swift. The last week in August they would begin to gather in their hundreds. The phone wires around the back of Lady Meadow Terrace would sag with their combined weight. Then the fantastic launch southwards following the Webburn valley. Disaster - 2019 nothing. Not a sign. Waited all through September for a later departure, nothing. Lots of guess work but no conclusions. Bit like shutting down Heathrow without a reason.

Every morning, after filling bird feeders, it has long been my habit to join them with a mug of tea. I can easily spend all morning sharing their lives.

With thanks to Beatrix Potter I have recorded a sample of my observations of the Berrywood Bird Table.

The Stage:

The Production

THE IMPORTANCE OF BEING HUNGRY

The Setting

Berrywood front garden, 7 am onwards

The Cast (at the start)

Sybil	Grey Squirrel
Crazy Gang	Flock of House Sparrows
Jack and Jill	Pair of Nuthatch
Walker	Male Blackbird
Oliver	Blue Tit
Mr Bulmer	Woodpecker *
Putin	Jackdaw
Marlon	Sparrowhawk
Aunt Ada & Uncle Arthur	Pair of Pigeons
Marilyn	Bullfinch

With guest appearances by

Long Tailed Tit
Marsh Tit
Goldfinch
Buzzard
Cuckoo

Selection of voles, moles and mice and Rusty ancient female ginger cat, complete with one tooth and large midriff

The action starts when I appear on the scene with containers of bird food. Already I have an audience – the Crazy Gang are cheering from their seclusion of the camelia bush. By the time I return with a mug of tea they are already squabbling for places on the feeders. Jack and Jill are next to arrive and in best acrobatic style proceed to breakfast upside down. As the Crazy Gang become quieter it is obvious that Marlon has arrived. He sits on the garden gate partly hidden by the lantern bush. No hurry as he surveys today's menu. A nervous Oliver arrives and hesitantly feeds whilst continually looking over his shoulder.

Rusty meanwhile sleeps at the foot of the feeder. She has become part of the scenery, no threat to bird life. Even odd seeds falling on her get no response. Next to appear is Walker. He walks all the way from his home behind the garage to the feeders. He does not join in with the 'cling-ons', but is happy to eat seeds that have been dropped. Marylin arrives and sits, showing off, on the roof of the bird table. Doesn't eat much, more of an exhibitionist.

MARLON

Then Marlon swoops in for his take-away. Marylin and company exit stage left and the Crazy Gang offer easy pickings. Marlon returns to the gate and gives his usual course in sparrow plucking. Peace and quiet quickly return. Ada and Arthur are now awake in the holly tree and commence serenading all of us with the most boring bird song ever. Bulmer has arrived, announced by his noisy drill on the fat balls (*John Bulmer was our family dentist for many years, with a great passion for drilling). Final bird on stage is Putin. He descends slowly from the conker tree and struts across the lawn. Not interested in bird seed, aggressive, single minded.

On the ground, below the bird table awaits the remnants of a Rugglestone Fish and Chip supper (*note from Kirsty – didn't think there were ever remnants from this!*). Sybil is sitting on it undisturbed, Walker dashes in and out for an odd chip. Putin struts towards this scenario, pauses for an eyeballing with Sybil. Walker, a bit of a

5

coward, scurries back to the garage wall. Sybil continues eating. Putin slowly advances, one eye on Sybil, one eye on Rusty. A scream and a spit from Sybil. A reluctant Putin retreats with only an empty chip bag for his efforts. From Lower Dunstone, the call of the cuckoo is the ideal accompaniment for Putin's retreat.

SYBIL

So gradually life returns to tranquillity. A few late arrivals; goldfinch, long tailed tit, marsh tit come and join us. Overhead a couple of buzzards are seeking larger take-aways than we can offer. By noon the site is deserted, apart from Rusty. Now mice and voles arrive to clean up dropped seed. Toothless Rusty now drops in and achieves results with her suffocation method. Minimum effort – maximum results.

Fresh Performance tomorrow….

Feeders full, cast assembling, audience comfortable with tea and toast. Weather dull and windy

0700 Curtain up

First on the stage as usual are Jack and Jill the Nuthatches. A brief appearance by Sybil who grabbed a stale doughnut and disappeared. Three Chaffinches are new on the scene. Perfect choreography, they move around the seed feeder in perfect unison. I have named them 'The Three Degrees'. They put on a show lasting an hour, non-stop in spite of the appearance of Marlon in the wings. The Crazy Gang has grown in numbers, must be almost 20 strong.

Marlon stretches a wing and the Gang scatter, some directly towards his perch. They have about as much directional sense as Attenborough's wildebeest. However, Marlon ignores them. Possibly changing today's menu. No sign of Marylin or Oliver. Maybe the Gang is too big a crowd. There is a queue gathering in the camelia bush.

A new cast member in the rotund shape of a robin struts around below the feeders. Very loud call, but no one is listening. Eventually he sits under the garden bench, sulking. A Captain Mainwaring character. Putin sits scowling in the beech tree, maybe one day he will get to play a bigger part. The extra noise of the large size Crazy Gang has woken Aunty and Uncle in the holly tree. They up the decibels in their cooing and our breakfast with bird song lacks harmony. Time to remove hearing aids. Marlon has also disappeared, maybe in search of more peaceful dining.

CAPTAIN MAINWARING

Mr Bulmer arrives and commences work on the fat balls. Today he has brought a friend who just sits in the Rowan observing the general scene. Does not approach the feeders, does not take a dig at the Rowan. Is he Mr. Bulmer's minder? Eyes moving but head quite still. Immaculate grey suit, smart waistcoat. I think Dirty Harry has joined us.

Eventually they depart, only a ten-minute visit. At ground level Walker struggles with a failed jam tart. A baking experience that was rejected by human beings. The jam had set hard, like strawberry superglue. This had now congealed around Walker's beak, whose vigorous efforts to wipe it off on the grass are not successful. Captain Mainwaring manages the pastry crust with no competition, but Putin can't be bothered, obviously suspecting a trap.

DIRTY HARRY

After one hour of steady eating, Jack and Jill and the Three Degrees depart. Uncle and Aunty have finally flown down to Lower Dunstone Barns where similar noisy relatives congregate. A few late arrivals, long tailed and marsh tit, but they only stay for a brief snack, then depart. Drifters!

Rusty has forsaken her bed below the bird table. Today she is sprawled out on top of a mole hill. I am intrigued in how this new tactic will work.

Curtain comes down as coffee and chocolate digestive biscuits arrive.

TRAGEDY!

Since Monday work has been carried out on a hedge close to Berrywood. This involved noisy machinery. Removing dead trees, making logs, hedge laying and fencing. On the plus side we now have views of the moorland beyond.

However, the downside is depressing.

No sign this week of Sybil the squirrel, who is probably homeless with her family. Also, no sign of Mr. Bulmer and his minder Dirty Harry. Uncle and Aunty are keeping very quiet in their holly tree penthouse. Marlon is also absent. Probably found a quieter take-away.

Jackdaw Putin now has a friend who sits a little lower and slightly behind him. They occasionally converse, trying to shout each other down. The lawn needs mowing and contains a lot of insects. Captain Mainwaring and Walker, in their quest for food, seem to be rehearsing for the 'Ministry of Silly Walks'.

Not much activity at the bird table. Regulars Jack and Jill are ever present, one hour of non-stop upside-down feasting. Little Oliver blue tit has returned with an even more nervous friend. Not naming this one yet, she may be just a casual pick-up. Jackdaw No.2 is now outshouting Putin for no apparent reason (Trump has arrived)

The last 20 minutes sees the usual arrival of the long-tailed and marsh tits. They have now become regular visitors, but their unusual relationship is puzzling. They both disappear and return at regular intervals. Possibly feeding rota. Always in the same direction – shrubbery overhanging the pond. Their togetherness makes them worthy of titles Morcombe and Wise. They certainly bring us sunshine. With the absence of Marlon, the Crazy Gang have extended their aerial display, even daring to swoop over the JCB. Marylin fails to appear again. Finally, the 3 chaffinches have multiplied and now number 5 in total. All on the same feeder. Excellent timing and footwork skills. Maybe this is the end of the 3 Degrees? We might be watching a can-can line up.

The machinery complete with terrifying sound effects has been again.

Peace is in Pieces

10

A late goldfinch has appeared on the bird table roof, then quickly departs. Rusty, stone deaf, sleeps on.

Hope for the environment – below the bird table and feeders fallen seeds are beginning to sprout. Strange greenery. Maybe try identification next week. The arrival of The Triffids would fit in with virus lockdown.

Murder Most Fowl

We were awoken at 6am by sounds of severe screeching from the Holly tree. I don't recall Holmes and Watson or even Poirot and Hastings rushing out doors to investigate clad only in pyjamas and bedroom slippers!

Too late, the deed was done. Uncle Arthur now very deceased on the garden path, partly covered in broken twigs and ivy leaves. Aunt Ada is still up the tree cooing softly and trying to gather together the remnants of a ruined nest. I am guessing the culprits are a pair of Magpies who came on a surprise visit yesterday afternoon. The only other suspects are a pair of Jays, who have also been surveying the garden this week. No signs of egg shells so can only presume that the pigeon chicks were the target. Uncle has been put to rest in the depths of the compost heap. Maybe Aunty will join the Lower Dunstone flock.

11

These are not happy times, with Sybil the squirrel and family apparently still homeless. The big log making and hedge laying is still in process but moving slowly over the hill and ever onwards. Our horizon is much changed.

Equipped with pen and paper (and tea and toast) I am ready. I decide that I should do a census check on the cast and dedicate the two and a half hour time slot until coffee break. The logging procedure could be creating other disturbances ???

Rusty	Ginger Cat	Sleeping
Sybil	The Squirrel	Gone
Crazy Gang	Sparrows	Present
Walker	Blackbird	Present
Mrs Walker	Blackbird	Present
Capt. Mainwaring	Robin	Present
Putin	Jackdaw	Present
Trump	Jackdaw	Absent
Mr Bulmer	Woodpecker	Absent
Dirty Harry	Woodpecker	Absent
Oliver	Blue Tit	Present
Aunty Ada	Pigeon	Present
Uncle Arthur	Pigeon	Deceased
Marlon	Sparrowhawk	Present
Marilyn	Bullfinch	Absent
Jack	Nuthatch	Absent
Jill	Nuthatch	Absent
Morecombe	Long-tailed Tit	Absent
Wise	Marsh Tit	Absent
3 Degrees	Chaffinch	Absent
Cheeky One	Wren	Present (new)

Cheeky Two	Wren	Present (new)
Gilbert	Thrush	Present (new)
Sullivan	Thrush	Present (new)
Visitor 1	Siskin	Present (new)
Visitor 2	Hedgehog (small)	Present (new)
Visitor 3	Hedgehog (large)	Present (new)

The list of absentees is quite puzzling. Is the logging destroying habitat or is it just the endless noise? Hopefully it is just noise disturbance and life will eventually return to normal. Walker no longer explores on his own, now always shadowed by Mrs. Walker. Capt. Mainwaring has taken over Miho's garden spade, continually jumping up and down between the blade and the handle trying to attract her attention. Marlon has departed. No sign of any plucking. The crazy gang never settle on the feeders longer than the count of ten then usual chaotic aerobatic display. Their visit to the feeders is their equivalent of a pit stop.

Jack and Jill's absence is very unusual, normally so regular. I hope it is only temporary. Also applies to the chaffinches, woodpeckers and tits. Marylin's absence I must consider as permanent, possibly Marlon knows the answer.

However, all is not bad news. Apart from Mrs Walker, we have seven new visitors. It remains to be seen if they are temporary or permanent. The two thrushes don't appear to feed. They just sit on the bird table roof and try to out sing each other. The table offered the remains of a Rugglestone pasty (*yet again amazed anything gets left from a Rugglestone meal, Ed Note*) but they were not interested. Just natural beautiful birdsong even overcomes the sounds of the logging.

The two wrens tested both feeders, the pasty and the fallen seed. Even tried toast crumbs on the picnic table. Never really settled, continually tasting everything.

A brief visit from a siskin who worked very hard on selecting the niger seed from the feeder. Tried the fat ball feeder but did not linger. Didn't seem bothered with the loud clashes from the loggers. Not happy with the pushing and shoving of the crazy gang. Also it could have been quite high on Marlon's menu. Quick exit.

Star attraction has been the arrival of a pair of hedgehogs, parent and baby. They were only slightly interested in the bird seed. Their favourite was some grated cheese left over from pizza making. When Putin joined them, they rolled up into a protective ball. Similar to the ostrich theory – if I can't see you, you can't see me! Eventually they uncurled and returned to an ancient woodpile. Assume this is home.

The curtain comes down on an interesting morning with Putin finally getting his beak into the Rugglestone pasty.

TRUMP

PUTIN

Meanwhile Rusty sleeps on, although she is almost hidden by the strange greenery that is appearing below the bird table.

Much has happened since the demise of Uncle Arthur last Friday.

14

On Saturday and Sunday we had a noisy gathering of wood pigeons in the holly tree, scene of the tragedy. Possibly Aunt Ada had organised a wake. It was very well supported. The garden path below the congregation had a very white covering by Monday morning. All is quiet now, so we presume Aunt Ada has gone to stay with friends in Lower Dunstone.

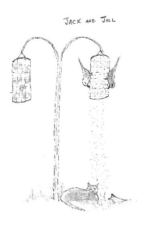

JACK AND JILL

Today the two wrens arrived with Jack and Jill, the nuthatches. Totally different behaviour. J & J like an old married couple, take up their usual places with their same routine, non-stop upside-down eating. The wrens are like two unruly children, unable to sit still, continually fidgeting. Oliver the blue tit arrives accompanied by a slightly larger blue tit. Both steady eaters with occasional glance over the shoulder. No worry! Not seen Marlon the sparrowhawk for a couple of weeks. I think his home is in the Bittleford area, so maybe he will appear on Wendy's list. She undoubtedly has a cuckoo that every morning enjoys a shouting contest with the Dunstone cuckoo. These noisy sessions are roughly at half hour intervals. Are they territorial?

Mr Bulmer, the woodpecker, is back on the fat balls, but no sign of Dirty Harry. An extra drilling sound is coming from a half dead sycamore in Dunstone Cottage garden, which may be him.

Jackdaws, Putin and Trump, have moved in a bit closer, now in our rowan tree. No action, just slight glaring.

MR BULMER

Captain Mainwaring, fat robin, no longer visits the feeding area. New parade ground in the vegetable garden, marching up and down between the rows of veg.

No sign of the crazy gang this week. Also not seen this season are the starlings. We really miss their non-stop chatter and psychedelic waistcoats. Where are they?

Gilbert and Sullivan, the thrushes, are now in competition with the Walker Family. The blackbird family has increased with an extra female. They appear to be engaged in a football match with the thrushes. Lots of short bursts of speed across the lawn, occasional quick insect snack. The ball is invisible but Mr Walker resplendent in his black uniform is the self-appointed referee. He always seems to keep himself between his two lady friends and Gilbert and Sullivan. Rusty has one eye open watching the action, a very bored CCTB.

Check on hedgehog refreshments. Last week's grated cheese not suitable, their diet should be dairy free. No visit this week.

The Three Degrees, chaffinches, have returned on to the fat balls and annoyed Mr. Bulmer. Lots of pushing and swearing.

No sign today of bullfinch or goldfinch or siskin but buzzard is circulating. Long-tailed and Marsh Tits arrive together again. Can't work out this peculiar relationship between Morecombe and Wise. Possibly live close to each other?

They don't stay long, brief performance on the seed feeder then exit stage left.

Bird table contains some bits of burnt bread pudding but no one is interested. The logging crew have disappeared over the horizon, peace has returned.

Sybil the squirrel and some shy members of her family are awaiting my departure. I can count maybe four plus Sybil in the beech tree.

At midday the bird table pudding becomes a contest between Sybil's family and Putin. Trump stays on the grass below the bird table, scavenging the droppings. Putin and Sybil fight over the big pieces. Finally, Sybil's family, after Putin's departure, move in for the remains of the day.

By midday the show is over and Rusty sleeps on.

THE THREE DEGREES

A few background events have happened since last Friday.

The Crazy Gang, re-enacting VE Day, tried to emulate the Red Arrows Display team. Performing in their usual chaotic style, they swooped over Marlon on the garden gate. The 'famous few' suddenly became one less. The day went totally unnoticed by the rest.

CRAZY GANG

Captain Mainwaring has become entrenched in the vegetable parade ground, and no longer visits the bird feeding area. Two other casual visitors this week were a yellowhammer (once) and a goldfinch (thrice). Maybe one of them will join the cast. Finally, since Sunday's proclamation by the Prime Minister, I am suspecting that my antics are under close scrutiny. Everyday, at various times, a drone is circling above Berrywood. It is disguised as a buzzard but lacks the distinctive 'meow-meow-meowwwww! Slapped wrist for MI5! No problem naming the intruder – BORIS

LooK.......
No EYES.

ST. DUNSTANS

BoRIS

Although today's effort is titled 'The Sad Tale of Toad Hole' don't be too disturbed, it has a happy ending!

7.00am Tea and toast at the ready. Props include a new issue of fat balls and a generous helping of sunflower hearts in today's seed feeders. Regretfully I have a serious cooking failure, unfit for human consumption. Although containing top quality pork sausages, my toad in the hole is a disaster. The batter set solid in a three inch thick lump resembling old builder's putty. This lies in waiting on the bird table.

Apart from the waste of good food, on the plus side I have observed unusual and interesting behaviour by my wildlife family. Perhaps other bird watchers would find this procedure worth considering.

First to arrive today were the crazy gang. Amazing how they recruit new members. Joyful abandoned flight. No Marlon yet. Walker is next to spring across the lawn with the two females in close attendance. Query – wife and mistress or daughter?

The Three Degrees have arrived on the fat balls, well spaced out, no room for visitors. Eric and Ernie have arrived together again. Apart from this strange pairing, I am unsure of Ernie's parentage. My new gift bird book suggests he may be a coal tit rather than a marsh tit. Nevertheless, it still remains an unusual partnership.

Jack and Jill get comfortable on the seeder and enjoy the sunflower hearts. No sign of Oliver or friend. Mr Bulmer has to get quite aggressive with the Three Degrees over fat ball space. One of them diverts to the seed feeder. Putin has crept into the rowan and is staring at the Toad in the Hole. Gilbert and Sullivan have already tried it unsuccessfully. Singing in a low key, they have descended to the lawn and joined the Walkers in bug hunting.

The Dunstone cuckoo has won the Town Crier competition. The Bittleford challenger has departed. Its solitary calling sounds quite sad. No sign of Trump or Putin but they are still both around with occasional appearances. I think Dirty Harry is still working on the old sycamore, heavy drilling.

Rusty is almost invisible in the strange greenery under the feeders. Can't identify them so might have to check special weed website. Possible business opportunity. Wrens one and two visit the table but didn't stay. Marlon stayed only for ten minutes then disappeared very quietly. No take-away today.

Sybil and some off spring are lurking in the wings. Since the logging episode she is very timid, only attends when I go indoors.

So lunch time arrives and the cast as usual, drift away.

The Toad in the Hole, which was being avoided, suddenly appears popular. From the kitchen window I observe Sybil arriving with two 'assistants'. A violent noise squabble now ensues. Rusty is woken and retires upstairs to the peace and comfort of the bathroom radiator.

The toad is refusing to be torn apart, the batter is resisting the battering. Sybil and her larger assistant are having a tug of war against each other whilst receiving some hard pecks from Putin. The small squirrel has decided the vacant fat ball feeder is a safer choice. Eventually the toad is upside down and claws and teeth break through. Sybil and partner scamper up the beech tree with huge lumps of heavy batter hindering their climbing ability. Putin steps in and with some heavy wing flapping gets the remainder to a lower branch on the rowan tree.

Conclusion – Sybil is re-united with Basil and still clinging to the fat balls must be Manuel.

The toad has a happy ending.

The rowan tree is now in full leaf and Putin has a new view point, top of the telegraph pole. No sign of Dirty Harry practising drill.

The three degrees plus two friends have taken over the fat balls. A problem awaits for Mr. Bulmer. Oliver and friend enjoying sunflower seeds – no sign yet of Marlon. Walker and partner seem to find loads of juicy bugs in the morning dew. The crazy gang seem to have divided into two squadrons. Taking turns, one group waits on the phone wire while the other performs. Short of discipline as occasional mid-flight diversion to feeder!

No sign of Eric and Ernie. Captain Mainwaring has taken leave of the vegetable patch and is tidying up fallen seed. No sign today of Walker's other 'friend'. Song thrushes Gilbert and Sullivan have not yet serenaded us. Too interested in the lawn bug hunt. Dawn was at 06.00 hours so maybe we missed the dawn chorus. Trump is flying backward and forward seeking somewhere to park.

MARYLIN

Marilyn makes her usual brief visit for a niger seed take-away. There are no burnt offerings this week as I have been presented with a new cook book.

Boris still hovers overhead. Just below him eight geese are trundling their way up the valley towards Natsworthy. A lot of large bird movement today. Already two jays and two magpies had paid a fleeting visit.

617 SQDN. 'THE DAMBUSTERS'

Jack and Jill arrive quite late for them. A third nuthatch is now sitting on the bird table roof. Maybe a youngster learning the ropes.

A squabble for space has broken out on the fat balls. Mr. Bulmer has arrived and hates being overlooked. The Three Degrees are not going quietly. Sybil has sneaked on to the scene, Basil and Manuel watching from beneath the wheel barrow. Bit disappointment – no burnt offerings. No fight with Putin.

Aunt Ada is back, gently cooing in the holly tree. Not building another nest, just a trip down memory lane.

Still no sign of Marlon, Oliver and friend have stayed most of the morning. A new visit by 3 greenfinches. Not interested in the sunflower/niger seed. My new book suggests that peanuts are their favourite. Add to shopping list. The noisy Three Degrees have departed.

Very late arrival, a Goldfinch, not hungry. Sits on bird table roof and sings very gently with a peaceful disposition. Even Bulmer paused drilling. Stays a long time but not feeding. All the other songsters do not join in. The only sound came from Putin, a half hearted squawk, which might have meant 'more'. She finally departs when Rusty stumbles in to life in pursuit of a butterfly. The plants appearing below the seed feeders are basically three different species. One is a very small sunflower, one is like meadow grass with seeds appearing, the third according to my wild flower book looks like the leaves of the dwarf mallow.

The bird table has quietened down, but surprise, surprise, the goldfinch has returned and is feeding, with only Jack and Jill for company. Strange habit of giving a little trill between mouthfuls. I think she will be a regular. I hope so. I think she fits the name 'Tracy'.

Focussed binoculars on Putin and I reckon he is smiling.

Nice to have a peaceful end for once.

PS Rusty did not get the butterfly.

My apologies for these lengthy surveys, but my garden lounger chair is opposite the bird table. Therefore my ramblings are a concentration of a day's activities – or even more.

Today at 0600 we were woken by Aunt Ada who has returned to the holly tree. With a newly acquired friend. She and he are now rehearsing for the Eurovision Song Contest. Non-stop cooing from breakfast until lunch time. No sign of nest building. At 0700 the seven geese do their daily fly-past. The leader continually squawks details of the local landmarks. A self appointed tour guide.

TRACEY

Tracy has become a very regular visitor. Must live very local, short absences then she returns to serenade us. Regardless of many distractions, she sings towards the heavens. Finally a mouthful of seed and makes a quick visit home. While she is gone the Dunstone cuckoo takes over. A very lonely call. Gradually the usual cast assemble. The fat ball feeder is missing! Undoubtedly the work of Sybil. It has been unhooked, dragged beneath the garden gate and jammed under a driveway marker stone. She must have had assistance from Basil and Manuel because all three were trying to break it open when we traced it. Tighter security is needed. Brinks comes to Berrywood, or are we an off-shoot of Hatton Garden?

Jack and Jill in their usual (or unusual) position. This week they have a single offspring with them. Eats much quicker, possibly teenage son.

Eric and Ernie have resumed their visits, sometimes individual appearances. No sign of extra partners, are they perhaps splitting up? Going their own ways, new horizons?

Marlon is on his usual gate perch. Not made a move yet. Seems to be enjoying Tracy's singing. A depleted Crazy Gang is also part of the audience. Maybe Marlon has already breakfasted and is just content to sit and listen. The Crazy Gang are very subdued. Possibly it is too hot for energetic flying.

Putin is on his new telegraph pole perch, occasionally shouts 'encore' to Tracey. Trump still flaps clumsily up and down the garden, unable to find a worthy perch. No sign of Dirty Harry pretending to drill the phone pole. However Mr. Bulmer is hard at work accompanied by a small assistant. She does no drilling but just sits in the shade of the bird table roof. She is more colourful than Mr. Bulmer and may be concerned about her make-up running.

Mr & Mrs Walker are pursuing their usual method of trotting and walking at the same time. Captain Mainwaring is annoying them by continually marching in front of them. He seems to consider all the lawn bugs are allocated to him. Bit of shouting and pushing.

The Three Degrees have not entered into competition with Mr. Bulmer. They are really enjoying the remnants of the frozen jelly which has slid off the bird table. It narrowly missed Rusty and is hidden amongst the strange birdseed jungle. Little Oliver shares the bird seed with his partner who we have named Annie. They both try to eat whilst watching Marlon. Not easy and a lot of fallen seed goes Rusty's way.

OLIVER

ANNIE

Fleeting visits from the siskin and Marylin. Siskin seems quite
selective and fussy about the seeds on offer. Casual interest only.
Marylin just has a couple pecks plus a bit of strutting on the bird table
roof. Always takes off when Tracy appears – jealousy?

The wrens are impossible to count. They are continually moving,
difficult to assess if there is more than one set of twins.

Strange happening last Saturday. A military chinook creeping up and
down the valley. Are they searching for lockdown escapees? Mystery

solved! Later that morning we are offering refuge to three greenfinches. No sound, no song, just filled up with extra rations. Penny dropped! Greenfinches is the name given by the Taliban to trainee jihad recruits. They have not shown up again. Research has identified the greenfinch as possibly Italy's No.1 terrorist. Specialising in the destruction of vineyards and orchards! Dark eyes, sharp eyebrows, they all have that Bin Laden look.

THE BIN LADEN THREE

Possibly our strawberry beds are under surveillance. Watch this space!

The thrushes seem to have found a new concert hall. Gilbert and Sullivan now sing at full volume from the beech tree that overlooks the bird table. Don't appear to be hungry, both in good shape but do love an audience.

GILBERT SULLIVAN

No burnt offerings for Putin and Sybil thanks to the new 'Easy Cooking' book. However Sybil and Co are already examining our two cobnut trees for early pickings. I may have to counter this by installing my personal alarm bell. Only problem is that Miho will probably come running with stretcher and first aid kit.

Finally the scandal currently hogging all branches of the media has reached the branches of Berrywood. Over the Bank Holiday we have observed a solitary gull hanging around. Perching on Dunstone Chapel. A long way from home. Only Putin seems interested. By Tuesday the gull headed south and has not been seen again. Considering that he has probably avoided Teignmouth Lockdown, it begs the questions, why just him?

All of this is happening underneath the high level hovering of Boris. Boris of course is just watching over Dunstone's inhabitants. The gull does not even rate a warning 'meooow'! Absolutely no doubt, this gull shall be named Dominc and Dunstone Chapel becomes Barnard Castle.

29

DOMINIC

The Berrywood Troupe (to date)

1	Ginger Cat	One tooth Rusty
3	Squirrels	Sybil – Basil – Manuel
2	Hedgehogs	Stan Laurel – Oliver Hardy
1	Frog	Michael Jackson
20	Sparrows	Crazy Gang
?	Wrens	The Uncountables
6	Geese	The Dambusters 617 Squadron
3	Woodpeckers	Mr. Bulmer – Dirty Harry – Little Wanda
3	Chaffinches	The Three Degrees
3	Pigeons	Uncle Arthur (decd) – Aunt Ada – Lodger
3	Nuthatch	Jack – Jill – Little Titch
3	Blackbirds	Mr Walker – Mrs Walker – Lady Friend
2	Robins	Captain Mainwaring – Sgt. Wilson
2	Blue Tits	Oliver – Annie
2	Jackdaws	Putin – Trump
2	Thrushes	Gilbert – Sullivan
1	Longtail Tit	Eric
1	Coal Tit	Ernie (change of parentage)
1	Bullfinch	Marylin
1	Goldfinch	Tracy

1	Sparrowhawk	Marlon
1	Buzzard	Boris
1	Gull	Dominic
3	Greenfinch	The Bin Laden Three
1	Cuckoo	Big Jessie
1	Great Tit	Idi Amin

Decided to strim down the strange growth beneath the bird table. It was restricting the ground feeders. A very colourful frog/toad emerged. Took a lot of energetic catching. Eventually returned to the pond. Michael Jackson reincarnated!

MICHAEL JACKSON

Mr Bulmer assisted by Wanda was already drilling at 0700. The four tits arrived over a 10 minute period, Eric and Ernie who seem to be friends again plus Oliver and Annie. A half empty seed feeder which had 'fallen' during the night finally found in the flower bed with the hedgehogs in attendance. As the sun gradually shone on the bed they shuffled off into the shade of the woodpile.

STAN LAUREL

OLIVER HARDY

Jack and Jill arrived with a nervous Little Titch. No Marlon yet. Tracy sings for her breakfast departs with a beak full and then returns to sing again. Putin as usual shouting encore from the pole top. Trump has a new far-off perch on the roof of Wind Tor cottage. Sybil sits in the shade of the garage trying to work on how to disconnect the fat balls from my newly installed bungie straps. Marlon arrives and Oliver and Annie depart. Tracy is not bothered, possibly someone is watching over her. Gilbert and Sullivan who were ground feeding near Marlon's gate perch have also departed. Background second class bird song from Aunt Ada and Lodger, and in the distance Big Jessie is cuckooing endlessly to no one in particular

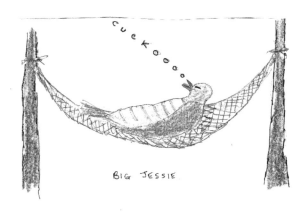

BIG JESSIE

32

The Crazy Gang seem to be teasing Marlon. Their fly pass route is at a very risky level. Haven't seen Marylin since Sunday. She seems to be on tour with the elusive siskin, just very brief visits. At ground level Mr and Mrs Walker are hoovering up big beak full of bugs covered in gravy dew. However this is not a peaceful meal. Capt. Mainwaring has today recruited an assistance. Mainwaring is now strutting and loudly abusing the Walkers but not getting much help from the new assistant. The assistant is quite content with turning over newly strimmed grass with an occasional pause but no conversation. Very peaceful robin. Sgt. Wilson by nature.

SGT. WILSON

Mainwaring sccms to have deserted the vegetable garden. Some frantic behaviour by the wren group, deep in the bramble hedge. Investigation discloses a solitary wren chick tangled in the undergrowth. Impossible to assist without cutting the hedge. Have to leave it to nature. I think it is even Marlon Proof. During one of Tracy's interludes, the Bin Laden Three arrive. From the bird table temple roof, one watches while the others grab a quick snack. All eyes skyward as the Dambusters plod their way up the valley. High above them Boris is slowly circling in total ignorance of the various dramas happening below. Very shortly the Bin Laden Three have taken on fresh supplies, a quick chirped message from The Koran and they are headed east to the great metropolis of Widecombe.

Whilst all of this distraction was happening Marlon has somehow acquired a meal. Too big to be a wren. After Marlon departed we found a few blue feathers. Have to wait until tomorrow to see if Oliver and Annie are still with us. Mr. Bulmer has given up on the fat balls and is attacking the phone pole. Can't be any life in it. Is he just trying to annoy Putin who is still sitting high above? Wanda is just sitting on the garage roof, but I can't believe she is going to learn anything from this unusual behaviour.

Tracy is back singing. Titch has decided to try the fat ball menu whilst Jack and Jill try to empty the seed feeder. As a family they seem to stick together, whereas Eric and Ernie keep taking beak fulls home and then return. Tracy sings on, completely undisturbed. She has become a very regular member of the cast. Maybe soon she will introduce some family members. Trump has gone, must have been hot sitting on that roof. No signs of The Three Degrees today. No sign of Dominic either, maybe that was just a guest appearance.

Mr. Bulmer and Wanda have finally departed. I regret to say that Putin and Sybil are unlucky today. No kitchen rejects to fight over. By midday most of the cast have dispersed apart from Tracy. However in the background the song pieces of Aunt Ada and Big Jessie are drowned out as Farmer Mann gathers his bleating sheep in for shearing.

Late Bulletin: Only six geese on the return to base. Why? Can't blame Marlon this time. Also sudden arrival of many wrens, completely out of control. Can equate these with a coach load from Dr. Barnardo's arriving at Dartmeet! So noisy! Even Tracy had to give up.

Sybil and Co are out again, late check on the cob nut development. Rusty's contribution to the day's events has been to bring a half dead mouse into the house. This sought refuge under the settee. Miho has now begun a late spring clean. Bird watching has some very strange side effects.

At dusk still the cuckoo can be heard, seems to be a permanent feature but only heard, not seen. Low profile immigrant – no passport – no visa. Late visit by a great tit. In spite of having a loud voice he is totally ignored. Lots of strutting and pushing. According to the book he has a second home in NW Europe. I think this is a misprint. Home is Uganda – Idi has arrived.

IDI ARMIN

Well, Dear Reader, this is the final draft on Berrywood bird life.

I have been persuaded to write some observations on the life of Rusty. She appeared unannounced last June. After considerable research (and vet fees) she is officially our property.

RUSTY

For the first few months she explored the house. Come the winter she set up a nest by the log fire. However with the coming of this hot dry summer she has developed a strange routine. She no longer comes in at night. She spends this time in the porch of Wind Tor, a holiday cottage which is 50 yds from us. This also happens when we go on shopping trips. Always comes home for feeding. We are inclined to think that possibly a holiday maker who stayed there last summer could be her parent family and she awaits their return. Obviously during lock down it has remained empty so she is not being enticed by extra food. The only query – did she get lost and miss her ride home or was she deliberately left behind? We will never know but some mysteries are best unsolved.

Obviously we organised her birthday party, which included salmon & chicken.

Bird activity has been difficult to record – so much is happening. Idi, the great tit has a partner. Both are overweight and unable to hang on to the feeders. They blunder about on the bird table over the odd crust. Loud arguments. Even the wrens could not find space to join in. Idi's friend is surely Cyril Smith. Maybe Marlon will fancy one of them when he finally shows up. Jack and Jill and Titch are already in action. Oliver, Annie, Eric and Ernie have all arrived. A friendly twitcher has confirmed Ernie is a coal tit. They are apparently good mixers and are noted for socialising with odd cousins. In the back ground Big Jessie sounds very half hearted, dozing on its favourite branch. Boris overhead has attracted a friend. Can't get their act together, one going clockwise t'other anti-clockwise. Has the Opposition turned up?

Marlon has arrived announced by a mass stampede of wrens and sparrows. Oliver and Annie still clinging on to what could be their last supper.

Aunt Ada and Lodger disappeared at the weekend. Right now probably in a Brighton B&B. Even Tracy has brought a friend. They tend to stay put a bit longer. The Three Degrees plus a friend have taken over the fat ball feeder. No sign of Mr. Bulmer and Co but he would struggle to find working space today.

Capt Mainwaring and Sgt. Wilson are on vegetable manoeuvres. Miho has been hoeing between the potatoes which is a great incentive to dig trenches. Mr and Mrs Walker don't seem so hungry today. Both are enjoying a dust bath. Putin and Trump plus a few hangers-on are up on the open moor. The remains of a lamb are being fought over. Watching through binoculars I feel more Rudyard Kipling than David Attenborough. The depleted Dambusters passed overhead, definitely down to six.

Gilbert and Sullivan now sing over in Wind Tor garden. They never trusted the sleeping Rusty. Two visits this morning by The Bin Laden Three. They share the same feeder as Jack and Jill but eat at a much quicker rate. Urgent business somewhere, always in a hurry. I think even Marlon would have his work cut out with them on the menu.

Sybil is watching from the roof of the garage awaiting kitchen rejects. Unlucky! Marlon had a quick dash across the bird table but came away empty handed. Wow! As usual the cast returned from hiding and commenced eating again. The Three Degrees did not return so the fat balls await the attention of Mr. Bulmer. The space was not vacant for long. Sybil tried to get at the fat balls so I had to deliver a shout of rebuke (or something similar).

Late afternoon, Tracey is still performing the Sound of Music in gentle harmony with new friend who I may name Selena. The Bid Laden Three have returned from that village, mission accomplished. Take on more supplies then head for the safety of Lower Town caves.

Also the six Dambusterss are safely heading back to their base at Stover. Good show chaps!

No Mr. Bulmer surgery today. Brief visit by a couple of nervous yellowhammers. I can understand why. Perched on Marlon's gate which has a visual display of plucked feathers below. They did not visit the feeders but departed quickly. On researching the feather collection spot some longer specimens. Could possibly be a long tail or great tit. Hope it is not Eric, preferably Idi or Cyril.

Closing up to the sounds of Big Jessie, the resident cuckoo. Still no starlings this year.

Fingers crossed we will witness the swallow/swift migration later in the summer.

Late, late extra. Miho spotted orange feathered friend passing by. Possibly a crossbill, too quick for me.

Post Script:

A bit of a dramatic sequel to keep you up to date. The relax in virus restrictions mean we can open our self-catering accommodation.

For the benefit of guests I put a bird feeder in the lantern tree, a new site, much enjoyed by the birds. Within 24 hours a new gang of squirrels appeared from Great Dunstone Farm area.

A total of six led by a reincarnation of Mrs Thatcher. Old residents, Sybil, Basil and Manuel put up a fight but were outnumbered and outfought. In spite of two separate feeder sites there was no offer of arbitration by Mrs. Thatcher. She and her gang dominated both feeders. Even Walker, who had shared space with Sybil was chased off.

Of course squirrel antics are a great source of entertainment for our visitors. That ruled out drastic action. Inspiration! I hung all the feeders on bungy straps. Thus leaping from branches on to the feeders ceased. The resulting bounces stop the Thatcher gang from clinging on. They hit the lawn in a very undignified manner. Putin, on his new view point the telegraph pole, breaks his deadpan expression and caws in approval. Mr & Mrs Walker are smirking from the garage roof.

Sadly though the only hope for the return of Sybil and family is a distraction for Mrs Thatcher.

If ever there was a need for Arthur Scargill to fly in now, finally, it is his time.